Beyond the Horizon

Written by Paul B. Mason

Illustrated by Lydia Sanchez

PEARSON

ISBN-13: 978-0-328-85392-2
ISBN-10: 0-328-85392-5

2 3 4 5 6 7 8 9 10 V0B4 19 18 17 16 15

Contents

Chapter One

"How long before you sail?" Sarah asked, dropping her eyes to the ground. She could feel the stare of the coachman, Henry, who sat at the front of her father's carriage, the faint shade of a smile on his lips. She could hear the impatient jangle of the reins on the horse's harness as she fixed her eyes on her father, dressed in his captain's uniform. Henry could feel the tension in the air and busied himself securing Sarah's father's traveling chest to the top of the carriage.

"Three or four days, if conditions favor us," her father said, glancing at the treetops bending in the wind.

"Three days," Sarah whispered. "And then how many years to follow?"

"I shall return before you know it, Sarah—why, I wager you and Aunt Mary will not miss me at all." Sarah's father smiled at the stern woman at his daughter's side, but she didn't smile back. Something as warm as a smile rarely graced Aunt Mary's face.

"My heart tells me differently," said Sarah, gripping her father's hand tightly. "Please take me with you."

Her father reached over and pushed a loose strand of golden hair behind Sarah's ear and ran his warm hand down her cheek. "Have we not trodden this path enough of late? You know India is no place for a girl, nor is the ocean."

"India sounds wondrous," said Sarah wistfully.

"It is a barbarous place, with barbarous people, mark my words. It is duty alone that drives me," Sarah's father insisted. He shook his head. "There is no more to be said."

"Then fare thee well," said Sarah, failing to keep the bitterness from her voice. "Go to your duty," she muttered.

"Let us not part on such terms, Sarah," her father whispered softly, his expression sinking. He bent down and kissed her on the cheek.

It wasn't until the coach disappeared over the hill and Aunt Mary ordered her to come inside that Sarah realized she had not even returned his kiss.

＊＊＊

With her father gone little more than a day, the
house became a tomb—dark clouds and rain drained
any remaining cheer. Sarah knew then that she had
to break free and follow her father or risk withering
away till there was nothing left of her. It was better
to take her chances at sea, she thought, and as she
pondered, a plan came to her. She would need to act
quickly though—her father's ship, the *Trades Increase*,
would soon be setting sail.

Henry's spare breeches and tunic were on the clothesline; he was taller than Sarah, and broader too, but they would do. Sarah also knew Henry left his shoes, doublet, and cap by the back door at night. She admired the fine doublet but it was too grand for her disguise. As she took the other clothes, she hoped he would forgive her. She would take the pennies left by her father and some bread and cheese from the kitchen, and that would be just enough to see her to Gravesend port.

Sarah cut her hair that night by the glow of the kitchen fire, hacking at it with a pair of shears. A part of her ached as she watched her locks drop to the floor, but she knew the golden shackles would hold her back. Lose them and she was unrecognizable, and that was what she needed to be. Sarah pushed what remained of her hair under Henry's cap, her neck suddenly seeming cold and bare. Henry's tunic smelled of earth and sweat, his breeches were loose, and his shoes were damp—not that any of that mattered. Grabbing her cloth bag, Sarah slipped the latch on the kitchen door without a sound and drifted out into the night. She quickly found the road and set off for the town. A coach to Gravesend would leave at daybreak.

Aunt Mary would figure out where she had gone, but by then it would be too late. Sarah doubted her aunt would shed a single tear.

✳ ✳ ✳

"But what do you know of cooking?" the cook of the *Trades Increase* asked, as he eyed the boy the bosun had sent his way. Standing there on the dock, the cook thought that the boy couldn't have been more than thirteen, and thin as well.

"I have helped the cook in the kitchen at home—I mean in my master's kitchen," Sarah corrected herself. "Pheasant, pies, roasts, and the like."

The cook chuckled. "Very grand, I warrant, but there's not much call for that on a voyage across the oceans."

"I need the work, sir," said Sarah, continuing, "I will prove myself, you'll see."

The cook shook his head. "You may soon wish you weren't on board—sailing to India is no fairy tale." He paused and thought for a moment.

A ginger cat swaggered toward Sarah through the
boxes and sacks on the wharf and rubbed against her
legs. She bent down to scratch him behind the ears,
and then looked up at the cook for his verdict. "Sir?"

"Very well, then," the cook relented. "But only
because we're sailing with the tide, and because
Tom here has taken a fancy to you," said the cook,
nodding toward the cat.

"Thank you, sir," Sarah beamed.

"Now come hither—what did you say your name was?"

"Sar—Sam," Sarah thought quickly.

"Well, Sam, let's give word to the mate. But you'd better not play the fool. Captain Booth's not one for fools." The cook gestured to the quarterdeck.

Sarah caught sight of the captain surveying the ship, a blue doublet done up against the wind, a sword by his side, his arms folded behind his back. She tried hard not to smile, but sure enough, it was her father conducting his final checks before they sailed for India.

* * *

Sarah was happy to know that the same waves that passed below her feet also passed beneath her father's feet, that they felt the same wind, that they faced the same peril. But life for the cook's boy was very different from that of the captain. Their paths rarely crossed, and when they did, Sarah kept her head down. She could not reveal herself on board the ship and weaken her father's authority.

Below decks it was damp and sticky, the stale air heavy with the breath of many men. Sarah shared their stench, their coughs, and their cries in the night. Her clothes became thick with dirt and grease. At least it wasn't hard for her to stay in disguise—none of the seamen washed. In their tiny galley, Sarah and Cook did what they could to provide good sustenance to the men. Their rations consisted of salted beef, and hardtack—the ship's biscuit, as hard as stone—and dripping and cheese, while supplies lasted.

Month after month passed: months of creaking wood, of rolling storms, of leaking planks, and a sickly feeling in the pit of the stomach. When the winds deserted them off the coast of Africa, they drifted aimlessly in the doldrums, the air becoming so thick they feared they would choke. Then they dropped anchor and took shelter for more months as wicked gales took it in turn to lash the convoy. The *Trades Increase* was forced to drop anchor several more times to stock up on water and provisions, and once for weeks on end to allow the carpenter to rebuild the rudder.

"At least this means we have fresh food for a change," said Captain Booth, eyeing the table one night as they lay off the coast of Madagascar. Lieutenant Armitage of the *Adventurer*, their sister ship, dined with the captain as Sarah stood at the door with a bowl in her hands, her eyes firmly fixed on the floorboards.

"That it does, Captain," agreed Armitage.

"Curse that infernal rudder all the same. Nearly a year has passed since we set sail, and our business has not yet even begun."

"The treaty and the land will be ours, sir," Armitage assured the captain. "All in good time."

"Let us hope so," sighed Captain Booth.

"Will that be all, Captain?" Sarah squeaked, barely raising her eyes.

Captain Booth paused for a moment. "Have we sailed together before, boy?" he asked, looking Sarah up and down.

"No, Captain," Sarah replied, keeping her voice as steady as she could. She dared not look her father in the eye. "This is my first time at sea," she whispered, her heart pounding.

"Then thank Cook for his troubles, boy," said Captain Booth, dismissing her. Sarah closed the cabin door behind her, leaving the captain and Armitage to their meal, and scuttled quickly back to the galley.

"What is this treaty the captain seeks?" Sarah asked back at the galley, telling Cook what she'd heard.

"The company has an eye to gaining land and setting up a factory—a proper trading post," said Cook, sitting with Tom on his lap as he watched Sarah clean the dishes. "The captain is seeking a treaty from the Mughal emperor himself; a piece of paper that says we can take from India what we please." Cook laughed. "He'll make this company a fortune—you mark my words."

Sarah thought for a moment and asked, "Do you think him a good man, Cook?"

"He can be a funny old cove, I'll warrant you that," said Cook. "But he's a rare and goodly captain, and I've sailed with a few."

Sarah turned her face for a moment, in case Cook saw her flush with pride. She found a piece of chewed beef on one of the plates and leaned over to feed it to Tom. "Well, I for one will be glad to get to India and get off this ship," she said.

"I proffered you'd feel that way," said Cook with a smile. "Now, be quick with those dishes, bilge rat!"

★★★

With favorable winds at its back, the *Trades Increase* crossed the Indian Ocean without further delay, and the crew arrived in India on September 14, a full year and three months since they had left the docks at Gravesend.

On the voyage, Sarah had watched from a distance how her father's hair had turned gray at the sides, and how his face had become creased and aged. She understood now why he had tried to protect her from the journey; men had dropped like flies aboard the *Trades Increase*, departing this life with scurvy or the flux, and the same was true of the *Adventurer*. Her father felt the burden.

As the shadow of India crept toward them over the horizon, Sarah could see the weight of these worries begin to lift from his shoulders. He was looking forward to the business and the days ahead, and with a flutter in her chest, Sarah realized that she was too.

Chapter Two

The *Trades Increase* sailed down the inlet from the sea toward the city of Surat, steering clear of the mangroves that threatened to block its way. Captain Booth gave orders for the ship to berth at one of the wharfs jutting out into the water. Alongside drifted the *Adventurer*, limping into the docks. There were other ships out in the harbor, all flying different colors, though none carried more guns than the *Trades Increase*.

Farther down the channel stood a fort, appearing to rise out of the water itself, with tall, rounded towers at its corners. Flags of dark green rippled in the breeze on top of tall turrets.

Clustered at each side were a straggle of wooden houses stacked side by side. They reminded Sarah of the crates in the hold. Beyond the city, dry plains stretched out into the distance, flickering in the heat.

"That's the Mughal emperor's," said Cook, nodding at the fort, "though his real palace is far from here."

Sarah gazed at the fort. "It's magical."

"If you say so," said Cook.

The *Trades Increase* didn't have much in the way of goods to unload, just some cases of unwrought metal and some wool, which Captain Booth intended to trade for fresh provisions. It was on the journey back that the hold would be packed to the gunwales.

"Once we have unloaded our freight, see that the men are paid some of what they are due and give them leave," Captain Booth told the first mate. "Set the curfew for seven bells, and have Cook and that boy of his seek out some good fare for our table tonight—something fresh."

Sarah and Cook walked the short street that ran alongside the docks, customers and stalls blocking their path at every turn, while dark-eyed cows wandered freely as if the street were their own. There were barrows with neatly stacked pyramids of fruits and vegetables— purple, orange, and yellow—like a sunset. In one barrow there were pale green strings; in another, bright red fingers. Sarah couldn't put a name to any of them.

Spice traders with white turbans coiled around their heads called out, their piles of bright powder pungent in the heat. Cook chose some fresh ginger, some little dark cloves, and a stick of sandalwood. "This will turn the captain's stew a lovely color," he remarked. Cook began haggling with the trader. "They'll have the clothes off your back if you let them, these locals," he muttered, wandering off to find a butcher.

Sarah felt something rub up against her leg. She flinched, thinking it was a rat, but it was the ship's cat, upright and proud.

"Tom!" Sarah gasped. "Whatever are you doing here?" she asked, scooping him up. "Naughty cat," she reprimanded. Sarah scanned the crowd for Cook to let him know she was going to take Tom back to the ship.

At that moment Tom sank his back claws into Sarah's arm and wriggled free, dropping to his feet. In a trice he was gone, weaving through the legs of people passing by and dashing down a side street. Sarah ran after him, her eyes fixed on the cat's tail. Tom fled through the muddle of streets, Sarah close behind, the buildings looming over them like cliffs.

"Tom!" Sarah yelled as she ran, her boots dusty, her shirt soaked through. Ahead, a mud wall blocked the end of the passageway. Sarah slowed down and allowed herself a smile. The chase ended here.

"Tom!" she called once again to the fleeing cat, bending down low in an attempt to gain his attention. Tom paused for a moment, to give his flight a second thought—wasn't she his companion who had fed him on board the ship? Then, with an unkind glance and a flash of his tail, he leaped up onto the wall and vanished again.

Sarah ran to the wall, fingers scrabbling at the baked earth as if to scale it herself, but it was hopeless; there was no way she was getting Tom back to the ship now.

It was then that it hit her—she had run blindly, and she had absolutely no idea where she was.

Sarah stumbled back down the passageway, turning this way and that, through the tangle of lanes as best she remembered. Chasing Tom was making it hard for her to breathe. At last she came across another person, an old woman sitting on the ground, sifting beans in a wicker basket. The woman glanced up at the strange *angrez* boy, her face blank. Sarah didn't remember passing her on the way into the maze of streets and lanes.

"The docks? Ships?" Sarah pointed down the passageway. "Ships?"

"Ji haa," said the woman, waggling her head and breaking into a smile. *"Bajaar, bajaar."* With her hands she showed Sarah to turn left and then right.

"Much obliged," Sarah gasped, relieved. Now she thought she could hear the sounds of the busy docks twisting their way through the winding passages.

Sarah picked up the pace once more, finally reaching the end of the alley. She turned left the way the old woman had said. She would be back on board the ship in no time; as for Tom, well, there were probably plenty of rats here to keep him busy.

As Sarah burst out of the gloom and into the light of the busy main street, she realized this wasn't the dock. It was a different part of the city, a different market altogether.

The heaving thoroughfare stretched for miles: a jumble of merchants and customers, of men in loin cloths with baskets above their heads, and bullock carts and barrows. There was endless confusion in every direction, and not a ship in sight, just a pulsing mass of people and animals. And above it all, a thousand voices, crying out, shouting, haggling, and not a word did she understand. The fear took hold of Sarah once again, and this time, she could not fight it.

Panicked, Sarah hurriedly chose a direction and pushed her way through the crowd, forcing her way along the thoroughfare. Expressionless faces stared at her. She spotted a man pulling a handcart down a street, branching off the main road. The cart was laden with crates—the sort she'd seen on the docks. Sarah ran after him.

It was then that the cart
flew into her, and the hub of a
spinning wheel smacked against
her head. Everything turned black.

Chapter Three

The eyes that stared down at Sarah were dark and curious. The girl had a purple headscarf, faded and worn, covering long black hair. In her nose was a tiny hoop of silver. She smiled to see that Sarah was awake.

Sarah was lying in a small room with mud walls. Light streamed in through an open doorway, and outside in the courtyard a water buffalo worked on some feed, its jaws grinding. Sarah recalled the market and the oncoming cart. But what of the *Trades Increase?* How long had she been lying there? Panic rose up through her chest again. Sarah felt her head where it ached and tried to sit up.

"Nahi," the girl wagged her finger, and gently pushed Sarah back down. She spoke to Sarah now, her voice dancing over an unfamiliar tongue, comforting, reassuring. *"Dadi!"* the girl called out, and an old woman shuffled in from the courtyard outside. In her hands were a bowl and a cup. The woman bent down and carefully lifted Sarah's head and put the cup to her lips.

"Pani," she explained.

Sarah took a long drink of water and lay back down. She felt so tired, so weak. The old woman ran her hand down Sarah's cheek with a soft smile, and Sarah thought back to how her father had done the same thing just before he'd left. She'd been so horrible to him; she wished he were there with her at that moment—she would react differently this time.

The old woman scooped what looked like brown mud from her bowl and smoothed it down on the lump on Sarah's head. The smell was overpowering—stronger than the spices in the market—but it felt cool and soothing, and Sarah's eyes began to close.

"Father," she murmured.

★★★

"What the blazes do you mean, *lost?*" Captain Booth looked up from the map that lay on the cabin table that he and Lieutenant Armitage had been studying.

Cook stared at his boots, cap in hand, the first mate by his side. "Yesterday when I went to the butcher's to get some meat, I turned around and Sam was gone, just vanished, Captain," Cook explained. "I thought he'd have come back by now."

Captain Booth slammed a fist onto the table. "I'll not see one of my crew forsaken. Send out some men—you go with them, Cook, and bring him back."

"Yes, Captain," said the mate, leaving the cabin.

"Foolish boy," said Captain Booth.

"We can't afford to let these tidings hold us up, unfortunate as they may be," said Armitage.

"I just hope he is found quickly," muttered Captain Booth.

Armitage turned back to the map. "This stretch of the channel just south of the town looks favorable for the trading post—a good approach from the sea and close to the trade routes to the North."

"Is the land occupied?" Captain Booth inquired.

Armitage peered at the map and shrugged. "A village or two, perchance, it matters not. Peasants can be persuaded to leave."

Captain Booth nodded. "Have your ship ready to sail. We weigh anchor tomorrow whether Cook's boy has returned or not."

★★★

The next day, when she woke up, it soon became clear to Sarah that her hope of making the *Trades Increase* before it set sail were slim and getting slimmer. Anguish washed over her in waves.

Her head hurt too much to move. Each time she tried to walk, blinding pains shot through her skull, forcing her to lie down. She could only manage a few steps at a time with her rescuer, whose name she'd learned was Priya, under one arm.

There was also the small matter of trying to figure out where she was. Priya helped Sarah outside and laid her down in the shade of a tree, making her comfortable. Then, while Dadi kneaded dough, Priya tended to a small fire. In the heat shimmering off the land, Sarah could just see the river—it was not too far from where she lay. Across green farmlands in the other direction, she thought she could detect the silhouette of a town. Was it the same place where the *Trades Increase* was docked?

Priya's home was no more than two rooms—
two mud huts in a small village of similar huts.
The huts all had curved, thatched roofs, and the
inside walls of each were smooth and straight.
Stuck to the outside were dark cakes made
of animal dung, perfectly flat and mixed
with straw, and each with the handprint
of the person who'd made it. Sarah
watched as Priya fed some dung
cakes into the fire as fuel.

"How did I get here?" Sarah asked finally, but Priya just smiled back. "Me . . . here," Sarah tried again as she pointed to herself and to the ground.

Priya thought for a moment, sweeping her hair behind her shoulder. Then she squatted beside Sarah and drew shapes in the dust. She drew a cart hitting a person and pointed at Sarah. Then she mimed carrying a weight and pointed at the water buffalo tethered next to the hut.

"So you put me on your water buffalo and brought me here?" asked Sarah.

Priya beamed, *"Ji haa."*

"Thank you," said Sarah, as she reached out and squeezed Priya's hand. Priya blushed. "What about my ship, the *Trades Increase?*" Sarah reached for a twig and in the dirt she sketched a ship with many sails.

Priya looked apologetic—she hadn't understood.
She called her grandmother over to look. They chatted
briefly but neither seemed to know what Sarah was
trying to say. Dadi gave Sarah a dish with what looked
like cooked spinach, and a flat piece of bread. She
raised her fingers to her lips. *"Khana,"* she said. Food—
Sarah suddenly realized just how hungry she was.

Sarah lay under the tree for much of the day, slipping in and out of sleep. Through half-opened eyes she watched as Priya swept the hard dirt outside her home with a broom made from twigs and tidied the rooms inside. Then she watched as Priya milked the glossy-skinned buffalo, tiny darts of milk slowly filling up her earthenware bowl.

Dadi sat next to Sarah sifting rice in a flat basket, picking out the bad husks and throwing them to the chickens that clucked and fussed around them.

Even though her heart was uneasy, Sarah couldn't help but think how peaceful things were here, how different from the life she had left behind on the ship. The huts made of warm earth, the dark-skinned girl with her headscarf and nose ring, and the lilting tongue she spoke in. These poor farmers had little, thought Sarah. They had no more than two rooms and a few animals, but they hadn't thought twice about rescuing a stranger from harm and taking care of her. They had saved her life; there was no doubt about it. Dadi had graced her with a remedy and kindness, and yet Sarah's father and the others thought them barbarous. How wrong they were.

43

By the afternoon, Sarah felt strong enough to get to her feet and help Priya collect water from the river. At the riverbank she watched as the other women went in to bathe, keeping themselves covered with their clothes. Sarah found a sheltered spot among some reeds and stripped down to her undershirt. It felt good to get clean. When she came out she noticed her clothes on the bank were gone, and in their place was a purple dress with a matching scarf, all made of simple cotton. A girl's dress—one of Priya's. So they weren't fooled by her boy's disguise after all. Sarah quickly changed; these were much better than Henry's ill-fitting clothes, which were caked in dirt. Now that she had a dress, she was glad she'd allowed her hair to grow a bit longer on the journey.

When Priya and the other women saw Sarah, they broke into giggles. *"Tum sundar ho,"* said Priya, her eyes bright. She was telling Sarah she looked beautiful.

At sunset Priya's father returned home, the baskets on the back of his cart empty. Sarah wondered if he'd been selling his vegetables in the city. Priya's father unharnessed his water buffalo and tethered it beside the other. Then he unraveled the cloth wrapped around his head while Priya brought him a bowl of water to wash in. Dadi busied herself making his dinner. Priya's father nodded at Sarah, and seemed pleased to see her dressed in one of his daughter's saris. For the first time, Sarah realized she hadn't seen Priya's mother—had she passed away, as Sarah's had?

Priya and her father talked while he rinsed his face, neck, and hands, and prepared himself to eat. Priya tried to find Sarah's drawing of a ship in the dirt to show her father. Sarah quickly drew another, and then she drew the coat of arms—two ships on a shield. She pointed at herself and then at the drawings.

Priya's father nodded; he understood. He put down his chapatti and slowly mimed the rolling of waves, the winding path of a ship.

In any language the meaning was clear—the ship had sailed. Sarah turned her head away and began to cry.

Chapter Four

The skiffs rowed toward the shore through the early morning mist, half a dozen boats with sailors under arms. Captain Booth and the sailors from the *Trades Increase* led the landing party, with Lieutenant Armitage and his men aboard the *Adventurer* close behind. The dark hulks of two ships kept watch from the water—great beasts, sailed from across the ocean.

Captain Booth's boat was the first to grind onto the soft bank, and two sailors jumped into the ankle-deep water to hold it fast. The captain stepped down from the bow, his hand on the scabbard of his sword. The shoreline was deserted. Apart from the rustling of reeds and the call of the water birds, it was quiet. The other boats made shore, and the men fanned out.

Armitage joined the captain. "Five fathoms by the mark as we rowed in. Soft sand—the channel will prove a good anchorage." He gestured at the water with the rolled-up maps in his hand. "We should look for a favorable stretch of land for a wharf."

Captain Booth nodded in agreement. "Let us tarry here and survey the coastline. Then we will head inland."

It was her turn. Sarah stood by a small circle drawn in the dirt. Around her in the clearing were Priya and her friends, laughter in their eyes—a strange *angrez* playing games with them brought lots of giggles. Sarah could see they were trying very hard to cheer her up. She managed to smile and pushed her headscarf onto her shoulders, sizing up the smooth stick in her hand, which she'd figured out was called a *danda*. On the ground was a smaller piece of wood cut to a rough point at both ends—the *gilli*. Sarah struck at one end as she'd seen the others do, sending the wood spinning upward. Then she swung as hard as she could. Wood met wood with a crack—and the *gilli* flew off across the clearing. The girls on the other team cried out. One of them jumped to try to catch it, but it was too high and it dropped safely to the dirt behind her.

Priya clapped her hands. Then she showed Sarah how to measure the distance from the circle to the *gilli*, flipping the *danda* end over end, the other girls watching on. Priya quickly tallied up the score. She and the other team captain, a girl named Abha, teased each other.

Sarah did her best to get rid of the frown on her face. Priya and her friends had embraced her— brought her into their lives. Each strike of the stick, each cheer, each laugh, meant that Sarah was one of them now, if she wanted to be. Sarah liked the village, with its thatched roofs, the smell of wood smoke, the low bellowing of the buffalo; but it wasn't home, and she wasn't sure what she should do.

With a loud cheer the game was won—Priya took Sarah's hands and danced a little because Sarah had scored the winning points. The girls said good-bye to the others and wandered back to Dadi. Sitting on the ground sifting rice once more, the old woman wagged a finger and pointed at the water jugs. The girls had some work to do. Then she beckoned to Sarah and fussed over her, raising the headscarf from Sarah's shoulders and draping it gently over her head.

Sarah watched as Priya balanced the round jug on her head, supporting it with a single hand. Sarah decided it was best to carry hers under her arm as she followed Priya down the dusty path to the river's edge. The girls had not traveled far past the village walls when they came to a halt.

Two hazy shapes lurked in the distance, on the water, masts proud—two ships. Priya had seen them too.

"Father!" Sarah gasped.

Then over the hill women came running from the direction of the ships, crying out in an anxious stream of words, their water jugs abandoned. Something was coming. Priya listened to them, and then she took Sarah's hand and pulled her back toward the village, following the others. The expression on her face said they needed to hurry.

Sarah broke free of her grasp. "It's my father's ship, I'm certain of it," she said, pointing to the water and then pointing to herself. Priya was confused.

"Priya!" There was a shout.

A group of men from the village came running through the fields behind them, led by Priya's father. In their hands they carried their tools, scythes, rakes, and hoes, gripped like weapons. Priya's father reached them, breathing hard, his eyes wild. He grasped his daughter by the shoulders and pleaded with her to hurry back to the village, his voice urgent, imploring, and worried. They were in danger. The villagers spread out over the path, tools in front of them, not sure what to expect coming over the hill.

"Captain Booth!" Lieutenant Armitage waited on the path for his captain. "The men say there is a village not far, and that some villagers ran off in alarm. Shall I have the men prepare arms?"

"We're not looking for a battle," Captain Booth grunted.

"As a precaution, sir? The Indians might not take kindly to us being on their land."

Captain Booth consented, "Very well, but only as a precaution."

Armitage gave the order.

The English continued their march forward from the ships, the path rising up a small hill. At the top the sailors slowed. Below them lay the village, little more than a cluster of feeble huts, and between them and the village gathered a gang of men wielding farming tools. The villagers cried out, rattling their weapons, warning them away.

Captain Booth gave the order to halt. "Stand fast, men!"

"We must let the Indians know we won't be discouraged, sir," said Armitage. "We should march on—I wager they will retreat."

"And if they don't?" Captain Booth asked. With their muskets and swords, the sailors could easily overwhelm the farmers, but that was not what Captain Booth wanted.

"That's their concern, not ours," said Armitage. "We will have the land regardless." He drew his sword and several of his men did the same.

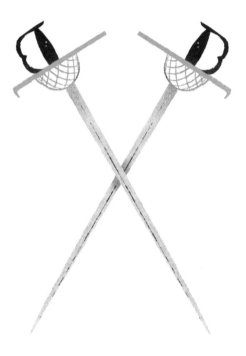

"Lower your swords!" Captain Booth snarled at the sailors. He looked at the farmers, their chests heaving with alarm, their eyes darting frantically. The farmers would stand their ground, Captain Booth could tell.

"Captain, we must not show weakness," said Armitage.

"Let us not be too hasty, Armitage. We will have land, but not like this," Captain Booth ordered.

Then there came a call from the crowd of villagers. A voice rose above the clamour, "Stop!"

Captain Booth and Armitage turned as a girl forced her way through from the back of the crowd. She wore a flowing dress, a purple top, and a headscarf. The girl dropped the headscarf, uncovering blond hair and fair skin. Silence descended upon the path.

Captain Booth gulped, his hands rising to his mouth. "Sarah?" he whispered through his fingers, hardly daring to say her name. *How could it be?*

Sarah stepped forward, "Yes, Father."

"But you're in England, with Aunt Mary . . ." Captain Booth's voice failed as he stared at her clothes, her face, and her short hair.

"I've been with you all along, closer than you know." Sarah felt tears build up in her eyes as she ran into his arms.

"Cook's boy?" Captain Booth gasped and Sarah nodded "But how have you ended up here?"

"An accident at the docks." Sarah felt for the bump on her head. "I was lost, but they saved me—my friends." She gestured to the villagers and said, "Please don't harm them or their homes."

"We must have our trading post," Armitage insisted impatiently.

"I implore you!" said Sarah. "Somewhere else, not here. Not these people."

Captain Booth thought for a moment and looked at the crowd. Priya's father and the others stood firm, and behind them near the village walls stood women and children. For the first time Captain Booth saw families, and saw that there was wood smoke coming from cooking fires, from homes. The captain nodded slowly. "My daughter is right," he said. "Our work is done for the day, Lieutenant Armitage."

"Yes, sir," said Armitage, his face red. He grudgingly ordered the men back to the boats. Sarah threw her arms back around her father and squeezed tight.

Sarah and her father followed Priya through the village back to her house to say their farewells. Sarah pointed out the clearing where they played *gilli-danda*. She showed him the cakes of dung in neat rows on the walls of the huts, and told how the villagers used them to fuel fires. She described the medicine that Dadi had put on the lump on her head and the kindness that the family had shown her.

Dadi was sitting in the shade of the tree with Priya's father, a tub full of milk at her feet. With her hands she pulled a rope back and forth, spinning a wooden churn. She bade Captain Booth and Sarah to sit with her, and they watched for a bit, listening to the twirling of the churn in Dadi's hands, the gentle sloshing of the milk. Then Priya fetched some cups.

"It's very pleasant," said Sarah's father, wiping the milk from his lips as he gestured to Dadi that he liked the drink.

"Dahi ki lassi," explained Priya.

"Dahi ki lassi," Captain Booth tried, his voice stumbling over the words. Sarah and the others chuckled, and Captain Booth chuckled with them. "Very pleasant indeed," he repeated, gazing around the village.

Saying good-bye to Priya was hardest of all. The girls stood together at the village walls, hands lightly touching as Sarah's father left them and walked back over the hill to the waiting boats. Priya had been her rescuer, her companion, the girl who had given her the very clothes off her back. Sarah thanked fate for giving her a chance to repay the debt—Priya's home was safe for the time being.

Sarah glanced at the ships in the distance, as if worried they would drift away with the current, and she'd be left behind once more.

Priya smiled and pointed at herself and then at Sarah. *"Dost,"* she said. *"Dost."*

Sarah understood her well enough. "Friends," she said. Sarah turned toward the path and took one last look back at her friend before running to the waiting ships, her purple headscarf trailing in the wind. For the first time in a long time Sarah felt calm—India had turned out to be a revelation in so many ways.